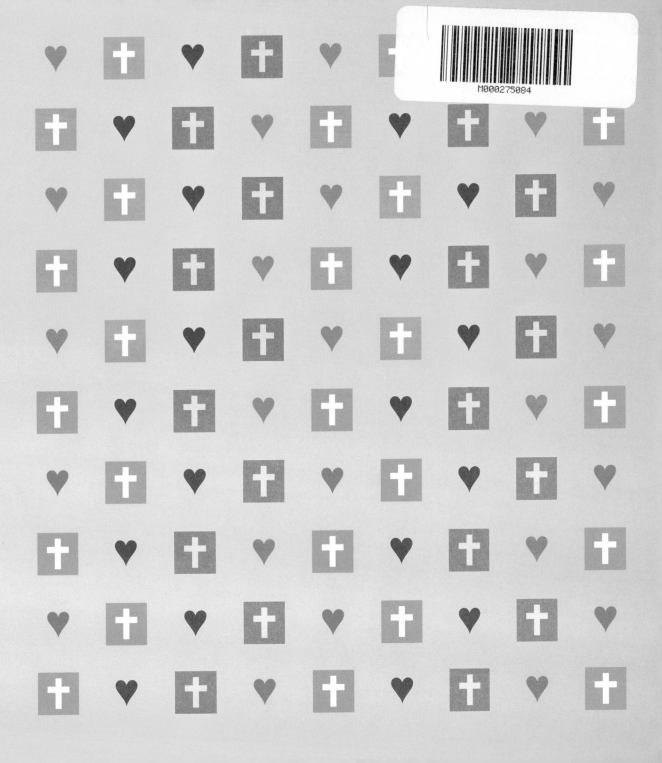

The CURIOUS Story of JONAH

Written by BOB HARTMAN   Illustrated by HONOR AYRES

ASCENSION
Kids

West Chester, PA

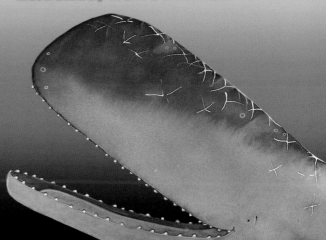

First edition 2014.
This edition published 2021 by Ascension Publishing Group, LLC.
Copyright © 2020 Anno Domini Publishing, www.ad-publishing.com.
Text copyright © 2014 Bob Hartman.
Illustrations copyright © 2014 Honor Ayres. All rights reserved.
Editorial review for Ascension by Amy Welborn.

Scripture passages are from the Revised Standard Version–Second Catholic
Edition © 2006 by the Division of Christian Education of the National
Council of the Churches of Christ in the United States of America.
Used by permission. All rights reserved.

Ascension
PO Box 1990, West Chester, PA 19380
1-800-376-0520
www.ascensionpress.com
ISBN 978-1-950784-79-0
Printed in the
United States of America

"Then Jonah prayed to the LORD his God
from the belly of the fish, saying,
'I called to the LORD, out of my distress,
and he answered me.'"

JONAH 2:1

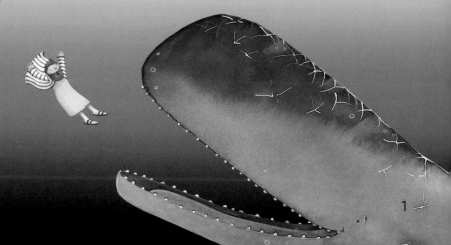

1

"The people of Nineveh have been very bad," said God to his prophet Jonah. "I should punish them. But I have decided, instead, to give them a second chance.

Go to them, Jonah, and tell them
that they need to change
their ways."

3

"I can't stand the people of Nineveh," Jonah grumbled to himself. "They're nasty bullies.

4

They make war on our people. And I wish God WOULD punish them." So Jonah went to Joppa, hopped on a boat, and sailed away in exactly the opposite direction!

Suddenly, out of nowhere, a storm blew up. The wind howled and the waves crashed and the boat was tossed up and down.

"I can't stand storms," Jonah grumbled, hanging on for dear life.

"Neither can we!" shouted the sailors. "Someone must have made some god somewhere very angry."

"It was me," Jonah grumbled.
"I worship the God who made
heaven and earth. He told me to go to Nineveh,
and we're sailing the other way. Drop me in the
ocean, and I'm sure the storm will stop."

The sailors didn't want to do it, but Jonah talked them into it. And when he hit the water, everything was calm again.

"I can't stand swimming," Jonah grumbled. "And it's a long way back ..."

11

And then Jonah
saw the great fish.

12

"I can't stand fish," Jonah grumbled. "And that is by far the biggest fish I have ever seen."

And before he knew it, the fish had swallowed Jonah whole.

GULP.

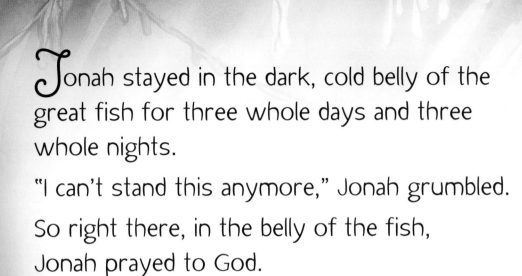

Jonah stayed in the dark, cold belly of the great fish for three whole days and three whole nights.

"I can't stand this anymore," Jonah grumbled.

So right there, in the belly of the fish, Jonah prayed to God.

"I disobeyed you, Lord, I admit it. But you have been good to me. I was drowning. I was doomed.

14

And then you sent this smelly fish to rescue me. So I'll do what you asked. I promise."

15

So God had the great fish spit Jonah out from its cold, dark belly into the light of day and onto the warm, safe shore.

Then Jonah went to Nineveh.
It took three days just to walk
across the city.

And everywhere he went,
Jonah shouted:

"God can't stand the things you're doing.
Change your ways,
or he will punish you!"

When the king of Nineveh heard about Jonah and the things he was shouting, he thought very hard and was very sorry. He dressed in something called sackcloth and sat in ashes to show God how sorry he was. Then he ordered everyone to tell God they were sorry, too.

The people of Nineveh all dressed in sackcloth just like the king. And they dressed their animals in sackcloth, too!

God was happy that the people had changed. And Jonah should have been happy, too.

But he wasn't.

"I knew God would forgive them," he grumbled. "He's caring and understanding and kind. But I still can't stand them!"

So Jonah went up a hill to wait and to watch, in the hopes that they would go back to their old ways and that God would punish them after all.

God grew a little plant for Jonah
to shade him from the hot sun.
Jonah was happy. But that night,
God sent a worm to kill the plant.

The next day, back in the hot sun,
Jonah (you guessed it!) grumbled.

"Why did you do that, God?
You know I can't stand the heat!"

"I know," said God. "But what I can't stand
is the lack of love in your heart, Jonah.
You care about what happens to the plant.

Fair enough. But there are thousands and thousands of people in that city down there who hardly know right from wrong.

I made them, and I love them. And I care about what happens to them."

"For I knew that you
are a gracious God

28

and merciful, slow to anger,
and abounding in mercy."

JONAH 4:2

THE CURIOUS STORY OF JONAH *ends here,*

BUT THERE'S MORE FOR YOU TO PONDER.

THE NEXT TIME GOD OR YOUR FAMILY NEEDS YOU,

WIILL YOU LET *your heart wander?*